THE
FOREST
IN OLD PHOTOGRAPHS
FROM THE DEAN HERITAGE MUSEUM COLLECTION

DEDICATION

To those whose labours have brought about a museum for the Forest of Dean

THE
FOREST
IN OLD PHOTOGRAPHS

FROM THE DEAN HERITAGE MUSEUM COLLECTION

COLLECTED BY
DAVID MULLIN

ALAN SUTTON
1988

Alan Sutton Publishing Limited
Brunswick Road · Gloucester

First published 1988

British Library Cataloguing in Publication Data

The Forest in old photographs from the
Dean Heritage Museum collection.
1. Dean, Forest of (England) — History
I. Mullin, David   II. Dean Heritage Museum
942.4'13   DA670.D25

ISBN 0 86299 410 1

Typesetting and origination by
Alan Sutton Publishing Limited.
Printed in Great Britain
by The Guernsey Press Company Ltd,
Guernsey, Channel Islands.

CONTENTS

INTRODUCTION 6

1 ALONG THE SEVERN VALLEY. AYLBURTON, LYDNEY, AWRE, BLAKENEY, NEWNHAM, WESTBURY. 9

2 HUNTLEY, MITCHELDEAN, LITTLEDEAN. 43

3 SOUTH FROM RUARDEAN. RUARDEAN, DRYBROOK, CINDERFORD, RUSPIDGE, SOUDLEY, PILLOWELL, WHITECROFT, PARKEND, CANNOP. 61

4 WEST OF CANNOP. BREAM, COALWAY, BROADWELL, JOYFORD, COLEFORD, STAUNTON, NEWLAND, ST. BRIAVELS. 111

5 LYDBROOK AND THE WYE. BISHOPSWOOD, LYDBROOK, SYMONDS YAT, REDBROOK. 131

6 HERE AND THERE. 143

PHOTOGRAPH CREDITS 160

L. WALKLEY, GENERAL CARRIER,
CINDERFORD AND GLOUCESTER.

INTRODUCTION

Photographers, both amateur and professional have been at work in the Forest of Dean for little more than a century. Their work in that time has left a detailed record which is a legacy for future generations. Photographs make history accessible to ordinary people in ways which documents and archaeological remains cannot. Photographs need much less by way of expert interpretation before they engage our interest and imagination. I hesitate to call the timespan covered by these pictures history, but some of the scenes have already passed beyond living memory. When looking at old photographs it is often the comparison between a familiar place then and now which first captures our attention. Many of the places pictured in this volume are changed almost beyond recognition. In other views we are surprised to find much that is familiar. Occasionally I have included more recent photographs which highlight particular aspects of this theme of continuity and change.

It is not just in modern times that Dean has been remade. Since people first occupied the land between the Severn and Wye they have lived by exploiting the resources which nature has provided, the woods and pastures, the iron, stone, and coal. In doing so they changed the Forest, but the Forest also shaped the character of its inhabitants. Over generations local knowledge, special skills and shared experience made Foresters of all who came to settle here – Celts, Romans, Saxons, Normans and their descendants. The Dean which we see in these photographs, at the height of its industrial development, is the product of their labours.

In Norman times it had been a Royal Forest, subject to special laws protecting the wild boar, deer and the trees which gave them shelter. Over the centuries of Crown control, ordinary Foresters were prevented from using the Forest as they wished. They were however able to establish customary rights, such as the right to pasture certain livestock in the woods and the Free Miners right to have gales for mining iron and coal granted exclusively to men born within the Hundred of St Briavels. In later times the hardwood trees, particularly oak, which grew in Dean supplied shipbuilding timber for the navy. This national need ensured that Dean remained a Crown woodland when other ancient forests were sold for farmland and enclosed. As the Forest survived so did the Foresters' rights, which remained vital to the livelihood of many people.

From time to time lax administration allowed the Foresters to greatly extend their use of the land. Many settlements consist of a scatter of cottages spread across a hillside. They owe their origin to illegal encroachments on Crown land. In earlier times Cromwell had the poor cabiners turned out of the Forest and had their homes destroyed. By the nineteenth century encroachments were so numerous and long established that eviction was no longer practical. Freeholds and leases were granted to legalise the position; from then on further encroachment was resisted, thereby preserving the distinctive pattern of many Forest communities.

At the beginning of the nineteenth century outsiders regarded the Foresters as a race apart. They were certainly a fiercely independent people: a sword belonging to a Free Miner bears an inscription which might stand as their motto, 'Miner against miner and miners against all other men'. The Forest was isolated by the Severn and the Wye. Roads throughout the country were poor, but especially so in the Forest, where the Crown opposed any improvements, fearing anything that might make tree stealing easier. The Forest lands were extra-parochial and so their inhabitants were free from inconveniences such as tithes, taxes and rates.

They were also without the benefits of organised religion or education. Into this wilderness ventured non-conformist preachers, who rapidly made converts, more than willing to testify to their former condition; a group of methodist colliers petitioned for the appointment of a minister in the following terms:

'Our state was once that of the lawless heathen, but now we have learned to fear God, honour the King and obey his laws. We no longer lay claim to his Majesty's timber or deer, nor do we attack and murder his keepers. The rising plantations grow unmolested and our neighbours flocks graze around us unassailed. We are no longer the terror of neighbouring towns, neither breaking their bones nor shedding their blood. Horrid blasphemies are changed into loud hozannas and instead of the lewd drunkards song we join in hymns of praise.'

The established church responded to the non-conformist challenge, building its first church within the Forest in 1813. Many other churches and chapels were to follow. Most had a school or school room attached. The proliferation of chapels of many different denominations continued into the present century. Sadly many of them, newly built when the photographs in this book were taken, are now disused and derelict.

The census of 1801 records 3325 people living in the Forest of Dean. Ninety years on this had grown to nearly 24000 and industry was at its peak. Its wealth was founded on two minerals, iron and coal. From the Middle Ages the mining of both had been governed by a complex series of customs under which locally born men

Free Miners – enjoyed a monopoly of mining rights under the Crown. Until the nineteenth century the pattern of working was characterised by many small shallow mines, close to the outcrop of coal or iron ore. When flooding or ventilation became a problem, mines were abandoned in favour of new workings. The greater part of Dean's riches lay deep beneath the surface. The development of beam engines for pumping and winding made deep mining technically possible, but the Free Miners lacked the necessary capital for such equipment. Wealthy Foreigners (outsiders) sought ways to circumvent the Free Miners' monopoly.

After a period of unrest in which the Free Miners resisted suggestions that their rights should be abolished, the system was reformed. In 1838 an Act of Parliament confirmed and defined the Free Miners' rights and laid down new rules, appropriate to modern conditions, for the working of mines in Dean. The Crown could still only grant a gale (the right to mine in a defined area) to a Free Miner, but the Free Miner could lease or sell the gale, once granted, to anyone he chose, Foreigners included. Very rapid expansion of both iron and coal mining followed. While some Free Miners prospered the dominant figures were outsiders such as Edward Protheroe and Henry Crawshay. Wealth was concentrated in few hands. Most Foresters lost a large measure of their economic independence.

In the early years of this century the iron industry declined, through exhaustion of the ore and competition from overseas, but coalmining continued to develop. New legislation in 1904 opened the way for new collieries to work the most inaccessible coal in Dean. These Collieries (among them Cannop, Eastern United and Northern United, pictured in this volume) provided work, as the great nineteenth-century mines, such as Lightmoor came to the end of their life. By the end of the Second World War it was apparent that even these recent collieries had a limited life. One by one the deep mines closed, the last being Northern United in 1965.

The change which this has brought about is different in character from anything which has gone before. New industries not dependent on the natural resources of the Forest now provide most of the local employment. Only a small number of Foresters maintain the Free Mining and Commoning traditions. For the rest the link with the land which has existed since people first lived here has been broken. A generation of Foresters has grown up to whom the woodlands are principally a place of recreation.

This book is intended to compliment the two previously published volumes of the Forest in old photographs, compiled by Humphrey Phelps. The photographs in this volume have been selected from the collections of the Dean Heritage Museum. In 1986 the Parkhouse collection was acquired by the museum after a successful public appeal to raise funds for the purchase. The majority of the photographs in this book are from this group of about 1400 photographs, mainly in postcard form. I would like to thank those who contributed to the success of that appeal and the many others who have placed old photographs on deposit with the Dean Heritage Museum. I would also like to thank the many people who have assisted and guided me in compiling this book.

David Mullin

Along the Severn Valley

NETHEREND, c. 1912.

AYLBURTON, c. 1910. Notice the handcart on the right, for deliveries from Woods Post Office and Stores.

The Cross, Aylburton.

Wood, Post Office, Aylburton.

THE CROSS, AYLBURTON, C. 1900. The cross shaft and the statues which filled the niches disappeared long ago. Since this photograph was taken the cross had been moved out of the way of traffic on the modern A48.

CHURCH LANE, AYLBURTON, C. 1910. Note the water supply pipe laid in the brook. An arrangement which is unlikely to have found favour with the public health authorities. The brook itself has since been culverted and covered over.

NASS HOUSE stands close to the Severn, east of Lydney. During the Civil War it was fortified by the Parliamentary forces laying siege to Whitecross Manor, home of Sir John De Wintour.

Lydney Park.

LYDNEY PARK HOUSE. After the destruction of Whitecross Manor House in the Civil War, Sir John De Wintour had a new home built nearby at Lydney Park. In 1723 this became the home of the Bathurst family who had the present house built in 1875 and subsequently demolished the old one. Behind the house lies a Roman Temple within an Iron Age Camp. Here iron-mines dating from the Roman period have been found.

AN EDWARDIAN NOVELTY CARD.

TWO VIEWS OF THE LYDNEY TIN-PLATE WORKS, which closed in 1957. Redbrook, Lydbrook, Parkend and Hawkwell near Cinderford also had tin-plate works. The sheets of iron for plating were produced by hot rolling; skilled and arduous work.

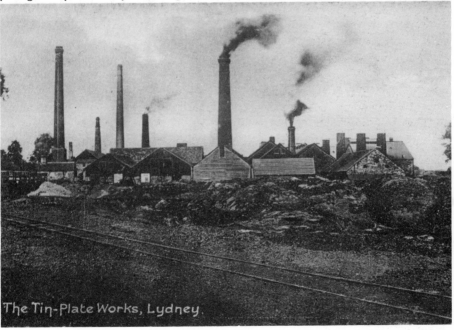

THE LOCK, LYDNEY, C. 1925. The lock, built in the early nineteenth century turned Lydney Pill from a tidal creek into a harbour basin. Goods for shipment were brought from the Forest on the Severn and Wye Railway, first built as a horse-drawn tramway. Notice the Crump Meadow Colliery wagons.

THE BASIN, LYDNEY HARBOUR, C. 1925, with Cannop Colliery wagons on the left.

The Docks, Lydney.

SEVERN TROWS AT LYDNEY in the early years of this century.

LYDNEY DOCKS in its heyday, crowded with many kinds of vessels. The tug is going astern. The tall structure left of centre is a chute on the quayside for loading coal from railway wagons.

Lydney. The Cross & High Street.

LYDNEY, THE CROSS, C. 1906. The house which stood on the north side of the square has been demolished, giving a good view of the Old Manor House which was probably an early home of the Wintour family. Work has begun on the Capital and Counties Bank building which now occupies the site. The horse-drawn wagon may have been delivering building materials. The Manor House itself was demolished twenty years ago and replaced by Wintour's Parade.

NEWERNE STREET, LYDNEY, c. 1910. The Co-operative Stores are on the left. In Lydney at least street lighting had arrived.

A MORE RECENT VIEW OF NEWERNE, but cars were still sufficiently infrequent to make crossing the road a gentle stroll.

HILL STREET, LYDNEY, 1934. The corner of the Railway Inn is on the left. Talking pictures had by now replaced silent films at the Albany Word Picture House.

FANCY DRESS outside the cinema, date and occasion unknown.

LYDNEY HIGH STREET, a post war view.

LYDNEY SWIMMING BATHS were a gift to the town from Viscount Bledisloe on the coming of age of his son Benjamin in 1920.

SECONDARY SCHOOLS, LYDNEY. The message on this postcard reads 'We are sitting in the cricket field belonging to this school watching a match between the boys and the wounded. It is a mixed school and adjoins the hospital.' The nearby Town Hall was used as a hospital during the First World War.

LYDNEY JUNCTION STATION, early morning, milk churns await collection.

THE TOWN HALL, LYDNEY, in use as a hospital during the Great War. This postcard was sent by a newly arrived patient to let his family know his whereabouts.

THE LYDNEY WAR MEMORIAL HOUSES, shortly after completion. The memorial bears the names of over 80 Lydney men who lost their lives in the Great War. After the Second World War a further 27 names were added.

THE LYDNEY OAK.

THE LYDNEY OAK, C. 1900. This ancient tree stood in Bathhurst Park. It was still showing some signs of life when this photograph was taken. The exact date of its disappearance has not been recorded.

LYDNEY AND AYLBURTON COTTAGE HOSPITAL, 1882.

LYDNEY AND DISTRICT COTTAGE HOSPITAL, successor to the above, approaching completion in 1908.

ALFRED ORPIN, coal merchants of Alvington celebrating their centenary in Lydney in 1936. Notice the whitewall tyres on the lorry.

Severn Banks below the Bridge

THE SEVERN RAILWAY BRIDGE, completed in 1879, linked the Severn and Wye Railway to Sharpness docks and the Midland Railway via Berkeley Road. Fragments of the stone viaduct are all that now survives.

THE SEVERN BRIDGE HOTEL, PURTON, c. 1920. Since the destruction of the rail bridge and the construction of the road crossing the prefix 'old' has been added to the hotel's name.

SALMON FISHING. One end of the long net is held by a man on shore while two others row out into the river, paying out the net as they go. The end in the boat is then passed to a fourth man on the shore and the encircled fish are caught as the net is landed.

STOP BOATS, with their nets raised. When fishing stop boats are held broadside to the current by cables anchored to the shore and river bed the net is spread between long poles called rimes. These are pivoted so that the head of the net may be lowered into the water. A salmon entering the net is trapped when the fisherman raises the rimes.

DRAKES' HOUSE, GATCOMBE, c. 1930. Strong local traditions link several Elizabethan sailors with the Forest. Arched openings allow the stop boats to pass beneath the South Wales Railway line (on the right) to reach the Severn.

AWRE STATION, looking north, c. 1914. In 1868 a junction was made here between the South Wales Railway and the Forest of Dean Central Railway, which failed to prosper.

AWRE CHURCH, c. 1905. This timeless scene seems remote from the Forest, yet in its churchyard stands the Crawshay tomb, a monument to one of the most powerful families of industrial proprietors in Dean.

BLAKENEY HILL, is typical of the many Forest settlements which owe their origin to illegal encroachment on Crown land by poor cottagers.

BUILDING TRADESMEN at the turn of the century. Notice the leather gaiters worn by the man holding the pocket book.

THE TUMP HOUSE INN, BLAKENEY, Landlord James Reeves.

CIDER MAKING, probably in Cottons Orchard, Blakeney. The motor driving the apple crusher is off to the left of the picture, but the drive belt may be seen. Among those in the picture are, from left to right: Maurice Willetts, Elsie Willetts, Sydney Willetts senior, Sydney Willetts junior and Walter Willetts. The dray which may be glimpsed in the background is similar to one now on display at the Dean Heritage Museum, which bears the Willetts' name.

BLAKENEY possesses one of the most pleasing roofscapes in the district, somewhat marred in recent years by the intrusion of concrete tiles. Samuel Hewlett, who owned ironworks at Soudley in the nineteenth century, is said to have had a hand in the design and building of the church.

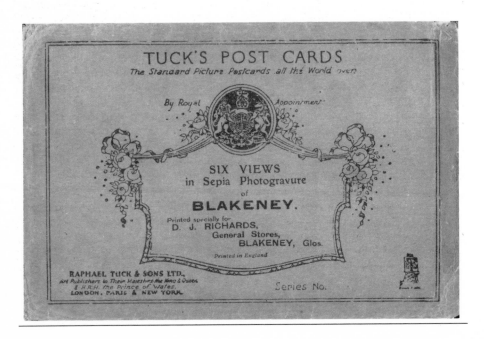

THE SQUARE, BLAKENEY. Although obviously taken in the early years of this century the occasion is unknown. On the back of the original someone has written 'Mr Thomas, Yew Tree Wagon sold out' The letters on the barrel are a joke 'O.I.O.U.R.M.T.'

OAKLANDS 1910. This was built in 1841 for Henry Crawshay, one of the incomers who made a considerable fortune from investment in the mines, railways and industries of Dean.

SPRING TIDE FLOODING.

HIGH STREET, NEWNHAM, C. 1920. Once an important town, Newnham was eclipsed by newer neighbours as industries in the Forest developed.

NEWNHAM FROM THE CHURCH TOWER, C. 1920. The Victoria Hotel is on the left. Horse-drawn and motor vehicles seem to have been sufficiently infrequent for the children to use the road as a playground.

STATION ROAD, NEWNHAM, c. 1910. The South Wales Railway swung away from the river to avoid the hill on which Newnham stands. A number of substantial houses were then built along the road to the station, no doubt some of the occupants commuted to work in Gloucester.

GLOUCESTERSHIRE. *Ten Minutes' Walk from Railway Station. Close to Church, Telegraph Office, and Doctor.*
TO BE SOLD (with immediate possession), A GENTLEMAN'S RESIDENCE,
Well suited for a SANATORIUM, BOARDING ESTABLISHMENT, or SCHOOL. Aspect S.E. and S. The Air is pure and invigorating, the locality being noted for Health and Scenery. Four Miles from the Forest of Dean, and within Driving Distance of Cheltenham, Gloucester, Chepstow, Monmouth, Ross, and many other Places of Interest.

BRIGHTLANDS HOUSE, sale particulars. It did indeed subsequently become a school. The Arlingham ferry is in the foreground.

The Ferry, Newnham, Glos.

S.D.
RealPhoto Series.

THE NEWNHAM TO ARLINGHAM FERRY. For many people living on the Arlingham peninsula Newnham was the most convenient place to shop and transact business, until the ferry service ceased after the Second World War.

RECREATION IN OAKLANDS PARK for Edwardian ladies and gentlemen.

THE CLOCK TOWER NEWNHAM. The inscription reads 'Erected by public subscription through the energy of S.W. Woods esquire. This stone was laid by Mrs William Crawshay, 2 September 1875.' The clock was renewed in 1956. In 1875 the Forest of Dean Colliers, many of whom worked in Mr William Crawshay's mines, were in a desperate condition, having been forced after a long strike to accept a 10 per cent reduction in wages.

NEWNHAM FOOTBALL TEAM. 23 March 1905.

Westbury-on-Severn.

WESTBURY ON SEVERN. In the Civil War, Royalist and Parliamentary forces fought for control of the church. The spire of the detached tower is roofed with shingles, it is said that in the seventeenth century shingles made from cider casks were used. The field gun stood on the verge between the two World Wars.

SECTION TWO

Huntley, Littledean, Mitcheldean

HUNTLEY, c. 1925. A fragment of a medieval cross survives elsewhere in the village. War memorials have replaced the preaching crosses of earlier centuries. This one bears the names of 21 who died in the Great War. After the Second World War two more names were added.

HUNTLEY CHURCH AND SCHOOL. In 1874 the school had 109 pupils, housed in one classroom. In 1875 the new school was built by the Reverend H. Miles at a cost of £2000. The tower is the only original feature of the church. The rest was rebuilt in 1862.

HUNTLEY CHURCH INTERIOR. Claimed to be one of the best churches by the Victorian architect, S.S. Teulon.

HUNTLEY 1914. This card is post marked 31 December 1914. The first Christmas of the Great War had just passed.

THE ROAD FROM HUNTLEY, C. 1914. Notice the newly laid hedge.

BRADLEYS GARAGE, HUNTLEY, C. 1930. The two men are Mr Harold Bradley and Mr Sid Green. The vehicles are a 1927 Austin Fabric Saloon and a 1926 Essex Super Six.

Mitcheldean from Court Field.

MITCHELDEAN FROM COURTFIELD. The George and the church are on the right. The brewery with its chimney is left of centre. This later became part of British Acoustic Films, then Rank Precision Industries. The post war expansion of Ranks in Mitcheldean provided much needed employment as the Forest Collieries closed down. The effects of major factory and housing development on Mitcheldean were not wholly beneficial.

HIGH STREET MITCHELDEAN, c. 1910.

FRED MASON'S BUTCHERS SHOP at the top of Hawker Hill, 1905.

MITCHELDEAN HIGH STREET, c. 1905.

MITCHELDEAN ROAD STATION, LEA, c. 1914, looking west. The Hereford, Ross and Gloucester Railway opened in 1855. From 1874 to 1878 a line from Whimsey near Cinderford was constructed to a junction at Mitcheldean Road. It was never opened to traffic and in 1917 most of the track was taken up.

MILE END MITCHELDEAN, c. 1905. Neither the exact date nor the destination of the machine being hauled by this traction engine are known. It obviously attracted some interest as it paused before the climb up towards the Stenders.

MITCHELDEAN BREWERY, devastated by fire in 1926. The brewery was begun in 1868 by Thomas Wintle, the Malthouse was built two years later. In 1923 Francis Wintle, son of Thomas put the business up for auction, at that time it supplied 72 tied houses. The site later became part of the Rank Xerox works.

PLUMP HILL SCHOOL GROUP V, 20 December 1926. Plump Hill School was built by the Forest of Dean School Board in 1878. The school boards were latecomers, following in the footsteps of the churches and chapels who first gave Foresters the opportunity of an education for their children. The former school buildings are now an annex of the Centre for Environmental Studies at the Wilderness.

A PLUMP HILL SUNDAY SCHOOL OUTING.

THE POINT PLUMP HILL, C. 1920. Notice the top of the limekilns by the road. The spoil heaps of the Westbury Brook iron-mine are spread over the hillside on the right.

CEMENT WORKS, MITCHELDEAN. "GLOSS" SERIES 1055.

THE MITCHELDEAN CEMENT WORKS. The view on the left dates from c. 1900, the photograph above is about ten years later. The works closed in 1919 after a life of about 25 years.

WIGPOOL IRON-MINE. In Roman times a road led from Wigpool to a large ironworking site near Bromsash and so it seems likely that iron-mining on Wigpool has a long history. By 1800 iron mining in Dean had all but ceased. Investment by 'Foreigners' (non Foresters) brought about a revival but exhaustion of the deposits, pumping costs and foreign competition have led to the extinction of iron-mining in Dean.

ST ANTHONY'S WELL, C. 1915.

A Forest Homestead.

A FOREST HOMESTEAD. All is not what it seems, this is in fact the upper mill of the Guns Mill complex. The pure water from St Anthony's well not only drove the waterwheel but was also essential to the fulling and papermaking processes which were carried on here. The slatted windows of the building on the right were to allow increased ventilation for paper drying.

VIEW FROM TEMPLE. BLAIZE BAILEY HILL. L4B.B.

HAYMAKING, near Littledean c. 1910.

BROAD STREET, LITTLEDEAN, outside the George, looking east. 'Ships yud row' (Sheep's Head Row), since demolished, is on the left.

GRANGE LANE, LITTLEDEAN. When this card was posted on 1 September 1939, Europe was'on the edge of war. Despite that upheaval and the intervening years this scene has hardly changed.

THE PRISON, LITTLEDEAN, c. 1910. This is one of four Houses of Correction in Gloucestershire built to embody the reforming ideas of Sir Onesiphorus Paul. In 1798 it replaced the debtors' prison in St Briavels Castle. In addition to a night cell each prisoner had a day cell where useful work was to be performed. Education and religious instruction also formed part of prison routine. As ideas of reform gave way to those of punishment a treadwheel was installed in 1842. The building was recently bought by an insurance company and is being converted to house a computer record store.

South from Ruardean

Ruardean from West End.

RUARDEAN FROM WEST END. With its Medieval manor site and church, Non-conformist chapels and coal-mine dirt tip, Ruardean takes its character both from farming and from industry.

THE LORD MAYORS SHOW, RUARDEAN, 26 April 1908. Behind the crowd are the premises of J. Linley and Sons, Carpenters, Joiners and Undertakers.

H. WEBB, LIBERAL CANDIDATE, for the Forest of Dean, 1911.

RUARDEAN CHURCH, two steeplejacks at work.

RUARDEAN CONGREGATIONAL CHURCH. Harvest festival, 4 October 1908.

BRASS BAND CONTEST, RUARDEAN FÊTE, C. 1910. Notice the loaded haywains and the long shadows cast by the evening sunshine.

BRASS BAND CONTEST, RUARDEAN FÊTE. The name Symonds may be discerned on the fairground wagon. Presumably the traction engine helped to haul the fairground equipment from place to place.

Ruardean Hill from Harrow Hill.

RUARDEAN HILL 1914. Encroachment settlements of long standing such as these were legalised by the Crown in c. 1835, when freeholds and leases were granted to occupiers. In earlier times Cromwell simply had their predecessors evicted and their cottages knocked down.

"Euroclydon" Drybrook.

EUROCLYDON, c. 1930. Built in the 1860s for Thomas Bennett Brain, it is said the tower was to enable him to see his colliery at Trafalgar. The house is named after a strong wind which blew a ship bearing St Paul from Palestine to Italy off course, (Acts 27:14).

DRYBROOK, 1908.

A PROCESSION AT NAILBRIDGE.

Forest Church & Vicarage.

THE HOLY TRINITY CHURCH, DRYBROOK, built in 1817, is almost the first evidence of the established church caring for the spiritual well being of the Foresters. The vicarage was for some years the home of the Reverend H.G. Nicholls, historian of the Forest and its people.

HAWKWELL ROW. Nineteenth-century workers' cottages on land released for building by the Crown. Lack of land for new housing in the Forest was a complaint of both workers and their employers as industry grew.

NORTHERN UNITED, May 1933. Ceremonies to mark the cutting of the first sod by Miss Liza Crawshay. This was the last deep mine to be sunk in Dean. The headframe came from New Bowson pit. Northern closed at Christmas 1965, leaving the remaining coal to the Free Miners once more.

Steam Mills & Schools nr. Cinderford

STEAM MILLS SCHOOL, C. 1915.

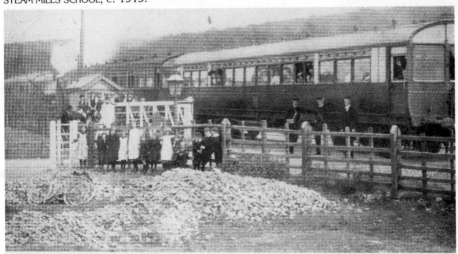

FOREST OF DEAN RAIL MOTOR SERVICE
STEAM MILLS CROSSING

Photo. by F. E. Jones, Cinderford

STEAM MILLS CROSSING, 1907. The autotrain service from Newnham was extended to Steam Mills on 3 August 1907. The trains took 30 minutes up and 29 minutes down.

HAWKWELL TIN-PLATE WORKS, after conversion to brickmaking in 1905. Handmade bricks were fired by means of fires lit in the arched openings around the domed kilns. The hot gases passed over the bricks before entering a flue beneath the kiln which lead to the chimney.

HAWKWELL BRICKWORKS 1987, one original kiln survives though long disused.

HANDMADE BRICKS ARE STILL PRODUCED AT HAWKWELL. The gas fired kiln is on rails. One stack of bricks is fired while another is made ready. The kiln is then moved to enclose the unfired bricks and the process is repeated.

THE TRIANGLE, CINDERFORD 1913. Westaway and Co. on the left.

THE TRIANGLE, CINDERFORD. Unveiling the war memorial. Relatives of the Fallen stand on the left, ex-servicemen on the right.

CINDERFORD HIGH STREET, Whit Monday 1909.

THE FOXES BRIDGE COLLIERY AMBULANCE CLASS, 1923.

WESTAWAY AND CO. PROVISION MERCHANTS, 1908.

THE VOLUNTEERS who built Cinderford Primitive Methodist Chapel schoolroom in 1908.

INTERIOR OF FOREST OF DEAN RAIL-MOTOR.

INSIDE THE FOREST OF DEAN AUTOTRAIN. The passenger service, begun in 1907, was withdrawn in 1958.

THE AUTOTRAIN CRASH, Bilson Yard 21 March 1914. Apparently the train passed a signal set against it, then passed over the points into a siding where it ploughed into the embankment.

EAST DEAN GRAMMAR SCHOOL, the domestic science room.

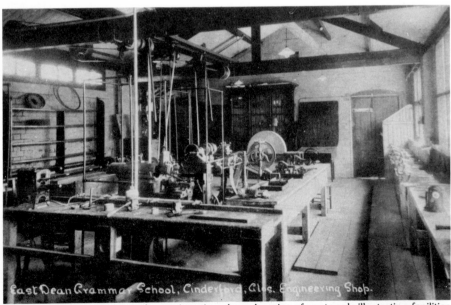

EAST DEAN GRAMMAR SCHOOL, the engineering shop. A series of postcards illustrating facilities at the school was produced, with the emphasis on practical and technical education.

KNIGHT AND CO. Auctioneers, valuers, agents and antique dealers. On 18 September 1914 Mr Knight sent this card to Mrs Lawrence of Longhope asking her to send him some apples.

THE DEAN FOREST CONTRACTING CO. CHARABANC.

PEMBROKE STREET, CINDERFORD.

CINDERFORD BRIDGE AND VALLEY ROAD, c. 1925. The Lightmoor Colliery tip is on the skyline with smoke from a chimney at the Colliery drifting over it.

CINDERFORD FROM RUSPIDGE 1912. St John's Church (built in 1844) stands upon the hill. The Bridge Inn is on the left. The tramway passed in front of the row of cottages on the right. The Wesleyan Chapel built in 1869 stands opposite the cottages.

THE VICARAGE, CINDERFORD, c. 1910.

NEAR RUSPIDGE HALT, looking east, c. 1910.

WORSFOLDS GARDEN, RUSPIDGE, one of the attractions available to tourists earlier this century.

RUSPIDGE, c. 1900.

RUSPIDGE, 1914. Compare this with the photograph above. In 1904 an Act of Parliament amalgamated over forty small coal gales to form seven large ones, with the intention of making them attractive to investors. Eastern United, begun in 1909 was one of the new collieries which resulted. The colliery closed on 30 January 1959.

THE SHAKEMANTLE IRON MINE, part of the Crawshay empire. The large building housed a beam engine. Coal for the boilers was tipped down the chute on the right from the tramway above. Some original prints of this photograph bear the incorrect caption 'Soudley Furnaces'.

SHAKEMANTLE LIMEKILNS, C. 1925. On the right a limekiln is working close to the abandoned Perseverance iron mine. To the left Shakemantle quarry has begun to develop.

FOREST-OF-DEAN, SOUDLEY VALLEY FROM ABBOT'S WOOD 450

SOUDLEY VALLEY FROM ABBOTS WOOD, C. 1935. Abbots Wood was granted to Flaxley Abbey in 1258 to supply fuel for their ironworks. The Blue Rock railway tunnel can be seen on the right.

SOUDLEY FROM BRADLEY HILL. 1905. No passenger service had yet been introduced on the railway line and so Soudley Halt, which stood to the east of the White Horse (which casts a shadow on the road), has not yet been constructed.

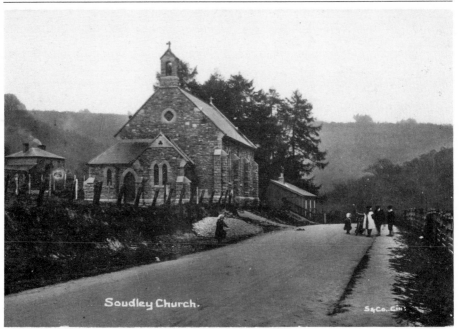

ST MICHAEL AND ALL ANGELS CHURCH, SOUDLEY, built in 1909.

ST MICHAELS CHURCH CHOIR, 1920.

SOUDLEY CHURCH GLEE PARTY, 1926.

SOUDLEY SCHOOL GROUP III, 1924.

THE ZION CHAPEL, SOUDLEY, c. 1910.

THE NEWLY BUILT ZION CHAPEL SCHOOL ROOM, 1 October 1914.

THE BRADLEY HILL TUNNEL, WEST PORTAL. The tunnel opened in 1854 and the track was converted to standard gauge in 1872.

SOUDLEY MILL, known as Camp Mill, built by James Constance in 1876 as a corn mill on the site of an earlier foundry. Note the sack hoist on the left.

CAMP MILL, C. 1906, after conversion by the Dulcote Leather Board Company. Later it became a saw mill.

CAMP MILL in decline, 1981, the buildings derelict, the pond filled in.

CAMP MILL refurbished, 1986, now housing the Dean Heritage Museum.

MINE VENTILATION CHIMNEY, STAPLE EDGE, c. 1910. The updraft produced by a fire lit at the base of this chimney drew stale air from the iron mines by means of a culvert going down into the workings.

PART OF THE DEAN ROAD NEAR SOUDLEY, *c.* 1910. Recent archaeological evidence has cast doubt on the local tradition of its Roman origin.

Denby Lodge, Forest of Dean.

DANBY LODGE, c. 1905. After 1668 the Forest was reserved for the growth of timber. It was divided into six walks, each with a lodge to house a Forester (meaning in this instance a Crown Official responsible for looking after the woods). The walks were named after prominent people (Danby, Latimer, York, Herbert, Worcester and Kings). The lodges have since been much rebuilt, partly due to the damage done to them by Foresters (inhabitants of the Forest) protesting at restrictions imposed on their use of the woods.

PILLOWELL AND YORKLEY SCHOOL PHOTOGRAPH.

PILLOWELL, c. 1910.

BAILEY HILL, YORKLEY, 1910. A pile of road-building stone stands on the left of the highway:

YORKLEY SLADE, c. 1935. The Methodist church is on the left. In the centre stand the newly built local authority houses.

LYDNEY ELECTRIC POWER STATION under construction in 1923.

LYDNEY POWER STATION burned coal supplied by conveyor from the nearby Norchard Colliery. Electricity was supplied to the Stroud area by means of a cable laid beneath the Severn. Norchard Colliery closed in 1957. In 1969 the power station was demolished. The site is now the car-park for the Norchard Steam Centre and Dean Forest Railway.

WHITECROFT, C. 1935. The New Inn stands a little way up the road.

PARKEND STATION, C. 1910. The roof of the ironworks engine house is just visible on the left. The chimney which dwarfed it has gone, dating this photograph to some time after 1908 when it was felled.

PARKEND, 1918.

PARKEND. The Severn and Wye main line is on the right. The former ironworks engine house has been converted to house a Forestry Training School. Outside the shop the newspaper billboards read 'Another Devalera Telegram', 'Dr Mags Threat to Trade Boards' and 'The wrestlers who want to stop.'

THE SPEECH HOUSE, built around 1674 as the Kings Walk Lodge, it became the home of the Verderers' Court. The Free Miners' court of Mine law also met here in its later life. Only the right-hand side of the building is original, the rest being added as hotel accommodation in 1883. Notice the two cannon on the right. These are believed to have been taken for scrap in the Second World War. One very similar bearing the Crawshay name now stands outside the Dog at Over.

A BEDROOM AT THE SPEECH HOUSE, c. 1900.

A SITTING ROOM AT THE SPEECH HOUSE, C. 1900.

A MONARCH OF THE WOODS DEAN FOREST.

AN ANCIENT OAK TREE, c. 1905. Oaks of this size are increasingly rare in Dean. This one probably began its life in the mid-seventeenth century. As the Forest is now well managed it is unlikely that many mature trees will be allowed to stand beyond their life span as a timber crop.

THE SPRUCE DRIVE, C. 1910. Contrary to popular belief conifers are not a recent introduction in Dean as these spruce, reaching maturity a decade before the formation of the Forestry Commission testify. Conifers have been planted in Dean since the late eighteenth century for timber, experimentally and for their landscape value.

AEROFILMS   CANNOP COLLIERY, FOREST OF DEAN   SERIES NO. 39912

CANNOP COLLIERY FROM THE AIR. Sinking began in 1906 and the colliery closed in 1960. Excessive water was always a problem. Some of the buildings are used as a Council depot and the workers houses remain. The railway has gone, trees are colonising the tip.

IN THE WOODS, NEAR THE SPEECH HOUSE.

CANNOP PONDS, c. 1935. These are man-made, originally to provide water for the Parkend ironworks, which once had the largest waterwheel in England. In the 1930s it was proposed to adapt them for boating and swimming if Dean was made a National Park.

THE CHEMICAL WORKS, SPEECH HOUSE ROAD, 1914. Here waste wood was charcoaled in enclosed chambers so that the fumes given off could be collected for distillation into various chemicals.

THE SPEECH HOUSE ROAD STATION.

SECTION FOUR

West of Cannop

FOREST-OF-DEAN. THE DEVIL'S CHAPEL

SCOWLES, THE DEVIL'S CHAPEL NEAR BREAM. The ancient outcrop iron-mines in the Forest are known as Scowles and some may date back to Roman times. They held a fascination for early photographers and many of their photographs survive.

BREAM, c. 1910. Notice the state of the road. Iron rimmed wheels quickly reduced road stone to a powder. In wet weather the surface was a thick slurry, when dry each passing vehicle raised a dust cloud.

THE INFANTS SCHOOL, BREAM, c. 1910.

BREAM THURSDAY CRICKET CLUB. 1910.

QUARRYING, c. 1905. In front of the steam crane runs a tramway of L shaped rails fixed to stone sleeper blocks. On it stands a bogie with cast iron flangeless wheels, used for carrying stone. The first railways in the Forest were horse-drawn tramways such as this. The main lines were converted to steam traction in the mid-nineteenth century, but several of the private branches survived as tramways well into the present century.

TWO VIEWS OF E.R. PAYNES' STONE WORKS, 1902. C.A.R. Bennett was Managing Director at this time. The sheds on the left house frame saws used for cutting the stone.

COALWAY CROSS, c. 1930. The Brittania public house stands on the crossroads, W. Bridge butchers shop is on the right.

BROADWELL LOOKING NORTH, C. 1925.

BROADWELL CHURCH AND SCHOOL, 1924. Broadwell looks anything but prosperous in these two photographs. The economic boom which followed the Great War soon collapsed and for many Forest communities the twenties were difficult times. The school was built as the Forest Church Jubilee School in 1863.

CANNOP HILL, BROADWELL.

LOOKING EAST DOWN HOWLERS SLADE.

JOYFORD HILL.

JOYFORD HILL, c. 1915.

Coleford
seems to be unrivalled for those
in need of "Change."

THE SEVERN AND WYE RAILWAY STATION, COLEFORD, opened 1875, closed 1967.

THE GREAT WESTERN RAILWAY STATION, COLEFORD, opened 1883. The stations of the rival railway companies stood side by side. The GWR line to Monmouth did not prosper and most of the track was taken up in 1916. The goods shed seen here survives and is being converted as a museum.

HIGH STREET, COLEFORD, c. 1905. The circus comes to town.

OUTSIDE THE ANGEL HOTEL, 1912. A Court Leet for Beating the Bounds of Staunton Manor. Mr J.W. Porter, newsagent, who published many fine photographs of the Forest in the early years of this century stands left of centre, wearing plus fours.

PROCESSION, COLEFORD, 1916. Notice that Unicorn House has a unicorn painted on the wall.

PROCESSION, COLEFORD, 1916. The VAD nursing car is passing the Town Hall.

COLEFORD TOWN HALL, C. 1910. Demolished in 1968.

SALTER AND SON, TAILORS. Their premises were on the corner of Boxbush Road.

THE ALMS HOUSES, COLEFORD.

Could you come up on Friday our high... are away I pray you... if you...

THE ALMS HOUSES, COLEFORD, 1889, newly built by Isaiah Trotter.

LAWNSTONE FAMILY & COMMERCIAL HOTEL.   G. HORWOOD, PROPRIETOR.

THE LAWNSTONE TEMPERANCE HOTEL, which closed in 1889. The building stands near the bottom of Cinderhill.

THE COLEFORD TRIPLETS.

STAUNTON, c. 1930.

J. W Porter, (Copyright)   THE SUCK-STONE, near STAUNTON (facing North).   Cole
The largest isolated block of conglomerate formation known, measuring 60ft. × 40ft. × 26ft. high.
Area of surface, 2,640 square feet.   Estimated to weigh over 14,000 tons.

THE SUCKSTONE, c. 1930. The Highmeadow Estate, in which the suckstone stands was bought by the Crown from the Gage family in 1817.

AN EDWARDIAN GARDEN FÊTE AT NEWLAND HOUSE.

F-DEAN, NEWLAND OAK

THE NEWLAND OAK, approaching the end of its life. It collapsed in 1955. It was one of the largest trees in England. Before it died, cuttings were propagated and a new Newland Oak, genetically identical to its predecessor is now growing on the same spot.

ALL SAINTS VICARAGE, NEWLAND.

ST BRIAVELS VILLAGE, C. 1927.

Lydbrook and the Wye

KERNE BRIDGE STATION, on the Ross to Monmouth Railway, was opened in 1873.

215 c   Railway Bridge over River Wye at Kerne Bridge.

THE RAILWAY BRIDGE AT KERNE BRIDGE. This bridge would have to be reinstated before proposals to reopen the railway from Chepstow to Ross could come to fruition. Notice the derelict cider mill on the left.

Bishops Wood Church.

ALL SAINTS CHURCH, BISHOPSWOOD.

BISHOPSWOOD POST OFFICE.

LYDBROOK HOUSE, for many years home of Dr McMinn.

VIADUCT HOUSE, LYDBROOK, c. 1910. Only the masonry abutments of the viaduct built in 1872 which towered above the house, now remain, the main spans were demolished in 1966.

MAYPOLE DANCING, Lydbrook Vicarage, 1913.

LYDBROOK PIERROT TROUPE.

OUTSIDE THE COURTFIELD ARMS, celebrating Queen Victoria's Diamond Jubilee.

LYDBROOK FLOWER SHOW, c. 1910.

Joys Green, Coronation. 1937.

JOYS GREEN, CORONATION DAY, 1937, celebrations at the Coppice organised by Mr Harding.

Lydbrook June 22. 1911

DONKEY CART, LYDBROOK, 1911.

LAYING THE FOUNDATION STONE, Lydbrook Primitive Methodist Church, 1912.

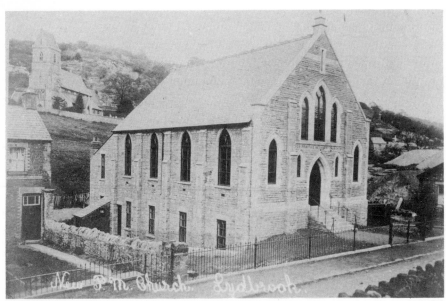

THE PRIMITIVE METHODIST CHURCH COMPLETED. On the hill behind stands the Church of Holy Jesus, built in 1851.

LYDBROOK RECREATION GROUND was constructed to provide work for local miners during the Depression. The Duke of Kent laid a foundation stone in November 1934.

THE LYDBROOK CABLE WORKS, built by Harold Smith in 1912. Wireworks are recorded in Dean from 1565 onwards. In World War I these works produced 70,000 miles of field telephone cable. Harold Smith went on to found Temco, which now has new premises in Cinderford.

Lydbrook Tin Plate Works.

Sorry not to have written, we
write a letter tomorrow, the
c. done splendidly. Bessie
came home on Sat., Give my
love to h when you see her
love from all . A.

LYDBROOK TIN-PLATE WORKS, C. 1908.

THE ROSS AND MONMOUTH RAILWAY where it enters the tunnel beneath Symonds Yat Rock.

201 c. Symonds Yat Station.

SYMONDS YAT STATION, C. 1905.

REDBROOK.

THE REDBROOK TRAMWAY INCLINE, C. 1908. The incline was built in 1812. The Wye Valley corn mill on the right was built around 1880 and destroyed by fire in 1919.

SECTION SIX

Here and There

THE BAND OF THE ROYAL FOREST OF DEAN BATTALION, GLOUCESTER REGIMENT. 1916. The reverse of this card bears the message 'Dear Hubert, just a few lines hoping to find you quite well. I will not be able to see you any more as we are going out on March 1st, but hope to see you someday. Yours ever Albert. I hope you will keep out of the army for my sake.'

MOUNTED POLICE IN THE FOREST, during the 1926 general strike.

GROUP OF MEN, c. 1910. The squatting stance of the men in the front row was habitually used by colliers in the confined spaces of the coal mines.

GROUP OF MEN, c. 1910.

THE OCCASION, date and exact location are all unknown. Notice the stone ware cider flagons.

A FOREST CHILDHOOD. From the shine on the car, it must have been a recent present.

AN UNIDENTIFIED CRICKETER. From its condition the bat would seem to be a veteran of many innings.

MR RON LANCASTER peeling the bark from a standing oak tree.

In Dean it was common practice to strip the bark from standing trees, using special tools. The strips of bark would be stacked to dry for some months before being despatched to the tanneries.

THE DEAN FOREST GUARDIAN is one local institution which is still very much alive.

A WAGON AND HORSES, C. 1910.

A RAILWAYMAN IN UNIFORM on his way to or from work.

A STUDIO PORTRAIT OF MARY JACKSON one of many members of the Womens Land Army Forestry Corps who came to train and work in Dean in World War II.

EXTRACTING TIMBER, WORLD WAR II. In the Great War the woodlands of Dean had been devastated for the war effort. Soon afterwards the Forestry Commission was established to create a strategic reserve of timber. In 1926 management of Dean and other Crown Woodlands was vested in the Commission. Before their work had time to bear fruit the woods were once again called upon to supply the needs of a wartime economy.

FORESTRY WORKERS, World War II.

TIMBER HAULAGE, World War II.

THE SWAN INN, c. 1905. Edwin Willetts was landlord.

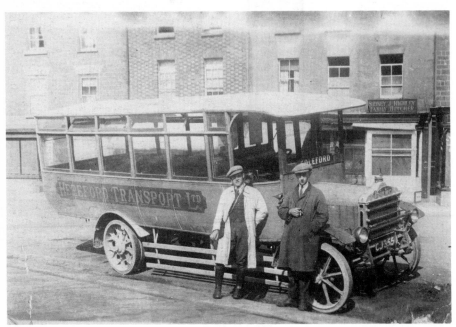

A HEREFORD TRANSPORT BUS, destination Coleford, 1922.